TAQUILA COLEMAN

PREGNANT *and* ALONE

*A single mother's guide
to navigating depression and pregnancy on your own!*

PREGNANT AND ALONE

A Single Mother's Guide to Navigating
Depression and Pregnancy on Your Own!

BY **TAQUILA COLEMAN**

ISBN: 9781070126302

TABLE OF CONTENTS

INTRODUCTION

"Where was this information at five years ago when I was going through this situation?" This was a comment left on one of the videos on my YouTube channel where I talked about how to heal after an abandonment during pregnancy. Just like she asked the question "Where was this information at …?" I, too, had the exact same question in 2014 when I found myself abandoned while pregnant. Stuff like this doesn't happen to me. I mean, you hear of guys not taking care of their child, but never in a million years would I have thought this would happen to me—not once but twice.

As I sat there alone, heartbroken, and depressed, I began to search the internet for answers to my questions, and to my surprise, I found none. I tried talking to my family and friends, and they told me to get over him and move on, that he'll come around later on down the line. That wasn't good enough for me. I needed to know, how could he just leave like this and turn his back on his own child? I mean, why was he being a father to his other children but not to mine? Why did the relationship have to end when I got pregnant? I had questions that I needed answers to, and I'm sure just like I had questions, you do too, and it's for this reason I wrote this guide—to help answer the questions you have in your mind and also help you get through this pregnancy alone.

I understand that there are some single mothers who want to go to therapy for healing but because of not having a baby sitter, a means of transportation, or money to afford it, they're unable to go. None of these things should stop you from receiving the healing you are searching for. Inside this guide, I share with you the healing process that has helped me heal from the breakup with my daughter's father and move on. You will discover why the breakup happens and how it's all going to work out for your good in the end. I want you to get excited because God has sent me here to encourage your spirit and to tell you, "It is not over for you!" God hears you. He sees what's been done to you, and He wants you to know that your season of being abandoned, rejected, and overlooked is over!

CHAPTER 1
WHAT TO DO IF YOU'RE PREGNANT AND YOUR BOYFRIEND WANTS YOU TO GET AN ABORTION

If you are currently pregnant, and your boyfriend is pressuring you into having an abortion, then the first thing to do is to remove yourself from the pressure by letting him know you need time to yourself. Determine the amount of time needed to help you clear your head and think about what it is you want. If he calls during this time, don't answer any of his calls or text messages, and if he just so happens to stop by, don't answer the door. Just like he's clear on what he wants, you, too, use this time to get clear on what it is you want.

So, what do you want? If the answer is "To keep the baby," then you stand your ground and keep your baby. Never allow a person to pressure you into having an abortion when what you really want is to keep your baby. You will only later regret it and also resent the person in the process. I didn't believe in having an abortion, and because of my own belief, I stood on that and kept telling my daughter's father, "I don't believe in having an abortion." Now, if he asks you, "What about giving the baby up for adoption?" Again, go back to square one: What do you want? Do you want to give your baby up for adoption? If not, don't! Because, at the end of the day, whatever decision you make will have to be a decision you can live with for the rest of your life. I fear God so much to stand before Him and tell Him why I aborted the baby He gave me, and I also can't live with myself knowing I gave my child up for adoption. And if he says something foolish such as "We'll be together if you get an abortion," then ask yourself, *Why do I have to kill his baby just for him to be with me?* Sounds like he'll only love you as long as you don't get pregnant. What happens next time you get pregnant? Are you going to have an abortion again? When will the cycle stop? When will he simply love you for you? Love has no condition. If he's putting you in the position of choosing him over the baby, then choose your baby and let him go. You can always get another man, but the opportunity of having another baby may not come again.

If you decide to keep your baby, and you tell him, prepare yourself; he will disappear and not support you. I'm not going to sit here and tell you to give him time or that he'll come around once you have the baby or all that other stuff you probably hear from your family and friends. I'm here to tell you the truth because I had been in your situation, not once but twice, and I don't want anything to take you by surprise. I'm a firm believer in listening to what a person tells you, and if he's already telling you that he doesn't want the baby, he's not going to support you if you have the baby, you trying to trap him and just want money, you're ruining his life, he's done having children, he has to get himself together, etc., whatever he says to you as to why he doesn't want you to have this baby, believe and listen to him.

"You're ruining my life": The truth is, his life was already ruined before you got pregnant. It just took you getting pregnant to cause him to take a closer look at his life, his lack of money, the job he either has or doesn't have, where he lives, and the type of car he's currently using. Now, if he looks at these things—the car, house, job, and the amount of money he's making—and realizes that it's not in the order he desires, he's going to see this baby as another responsibility that he doesn't want to deal with, and for this reason, he asks for an abortion. Don't feel sorry for him, and whatever you do, don't start thinking like him—seeing the baby as a burden. Children are a blessing from the Lord, according to Psalm 127:3. So, if the Lord your God has blessed your womb with a child, then thank Him by having the baby.

"You're trying to trap me and just want money": Girl, you got yourself an immature boy on your hands. Immature boys don't take responsibility for their actions. It takes two people to make a baby, and if he knew he didn't want any kid, then he shouldn't have had sex with you. It's not your fault that he couldn't control his sexual urges around you. I met a man who was very attracted to me and was also clear about not being someone's baby daddy but a husband to one woman, and for this reason, he practiced self-control and self-discipline and also put boundaries in place to keep us from slipping up and having sex.

"I have to get myself together": He could be telling you the truth here, except not going into details as to what getting himself together really means. He probably already knows he isn't right, he's no good, sleeping with five other women on the side that you know nothing about, and so many other things. Whatever the case may be, it is his responsibility to get himself together whenever he chooses, but in the meantime, you keep your baby.

Do you see how all of his excuses have nothing to do with you or the baby but everything to do with him?

Now, if he decides to leave and stops talking to you, this will hurt, and you will have a hard time trying to wrap your brain around how this man you loved could do this to you. Here's where you must pay attention because God is showing you what he is really built on. His foundation is that of lies, deceit, control, manipulation, anger, rage, and abandonment. You thought he was the man of your dreams, and you wanted to get married to him and spend the rest of your life with him, but what you didn't know was how he responds under pressure. Now you know. What you didn't know was how he really felt about you. You didn't know about his other women on the side because you thought you were his one and only. God is giving you the chance to see him for who he really is, a broken man that needs God. And if you're wondering if this is God's plan to cause him to leave you with a child, then the answer is no. Since the very beginning, God had family in mind when He created Adam and Eve and gave them the instruction to be fruitful and fill the earth. It's never in God's plan to cause any man to abandon his child, but God will use his leaving for your good. You just have to trust the process and know that even when man leaves you, God stays by your side.

CHAPTER 2
YOUR SEASON OF BEING ABANDONED AND REJECTED IS OVER!

Isaiah 43:19 says, "See, I am doing a new thing! Now it springs up; do you not perceive it?" It's hard to see what God is doing in all of this. "Why me? Why does my child have to grow up without a father?" Right now, you're probably feeling like life is unfair, and he's getting away with what he's done to you, but I'm here to encourage you by saying, "Do not be deceived; God cannot be mocked. A man reaps what he sows. The one who sows to please his sinful nature, from that nature will reap destruction; the one who sows to please the Spirit, from the Spirit will reap eternal life" (Galatians 6:7–8). He may have left and turned his back on you and the baby and moved on to another woman, but best believe God will give him no rest until he turns from his wicked ways, repents before God, and comes back to do right by you and his child. Until then, let's talk about the new thing God is doing.

From this moment on, I want you to start seeing the breakup as the blessing. The breakup had to happen so that it breaks you off your old self and ushers you into your new you. Immediately after the breakup with my daughter's father, I got before God and just dwelt in His presence because I felt so rejected and unwanted by everyone I didn't know what else to do other than get before God and just pour my heart out to Him and hope and pray that He heals my heart and takes away the pain. In the presence of God, I found peace and clarity. God led me to the book *Healing the Orphan Spirit* by Leif Hetland, and upon reading the first chapter, I knew exactly what was going on in my life and why life as a single mom is a hard one.

The Orphan Spirit

Now, we know an orphan is a child whose parents are dead. God revealed to me through Leif Hetland's book that spiritually, I was operating from the mindset of an orphan. What does that mean? A spiritual orphan is one who's familiar with fear, rejection, abandonment, being homeless, having no friends, and even though both parents are alive, there's no connection or love between the parents and the child.

From the age of 14, I started noticing the problems that existed between my mother and me. She showed signs of jealousy, was very cold and hateful toward me but nice and loving to my brother. At times, I felt her competing with me and couldn't understand why. She placed me in a situation to get abused and mistreated by others and then later turned the abuse back onto me to prevent her from taking responsibility for not protecting me as a child. My father was in my life but not available emotionally. Out of his mouth, he said, "I love you," but his action showed he could care less about his daughter. I felt no protection from my father. I never heard the words "I'm proud of you, daughter." As a result, I began to take on an orphan spirit, trying to figure life out on my own. I turned to men for love and protection but found the opposite—hurt and rejection. As I began to read the book *Healing the Orphan Spirit*, more revelation about my life began to unfold, and I believe it's for this reason God placed it in my heart to write this book.

God wants to heal you from the spirit of an orphan. It was never in God's plan for His daughters, single mothers, to raise children without fathers. From the very beginning, God had family in mind. When He created Adam and Eve, He told them, "Be fruitful and increase in number; fill the earth and subdue it." But we often ignore the red flags we see early on in the relationship with our children's father. Satan creeps in, causing distortion to happen in the father's mind, causing him to have thoughts such as "You got pregnant on purpose," "You're trying to trap me," or "You're ruining my life." These thoughts keep them out of their children's lives. Then when he leaves, and we look to our family for support, and it's non-existent, we're forced to feel like we're all alone with no help or support. It's no wonder single mothers are finding themselves depressed and feeling hopeless about their situation; everyone has given up on them. So, what do you do in a situation like this? Turn to God for help, support, healing, and restoration.

Allow me to encourage you by saying that God is not punishing you because you had a baby out of wedlock. Life is hard right now because that's how God disciplines those He loves. The hardship is there to build you, not break you. God does not desire for you to work two, three, or even four jobs just to make ends meet. This was never the plan for His daughters. God wants to place you in a land called Jireh, but for Him to do this, you must get to know Him as your Father. Right now, you probably view God in the same light as your parents. If your father abandoned you, and you were the one who always reached out to him to keep the father-daughter connection going, then this is how you will view God. This is why you believe God is punishing you for getting pregnant out of wedlock. Hence when you take a look at your relationship with your mother, the jealousy, abuse, and mistreatment make you feel as if you're never enough. You begin to think you must be a mistake and begin to question to God why He even created you in the first place. This is what God wants to heal you from, all of what you had been exposed to and the way you think about Him, yourself, and the way you're currently living your life.

Healing the orphan spirit can only be achieved in the presence of God—by having a personal encounter with God. In 2018, God told me that He would use my life as a testimony to set the captives free. I'm very impatient; when God tells me something, I often expect to see it happen the next day. So, as months went by, and I still found myself struggling financially and suffering from depression, I became frustrated and said to God, "How am I going to help single mothers when I'm struggling too?" That day, I prayed and asked God to give me a personal encounter with Him so that I know Him to be real in my life and I have a major testimony to share about God. That same year, in October of 2018, I was suddenly evicted from my two-bedroom condo. Now, the good thing about God and the eviction was that three months before the eviction, God had instructed me to start looking for hotels to stay at because our next move was going to be sudden. And just like that, my children and I would be living in a different place.

When I came home after dropping off my son at school, I saw the eviction letter taped to the door. I opened the letter; it said that I had seven days to either pay the rent that was due or leave. I said to my oldest son, "Take what you want; we're going to leave the rest here. We're moving tomorrow." We both were happy but also shocked at the same time. Our current environment was an environment of oppression. I constantly felt beat down, depressed, and under attack. That environment was very toxic and unhealthy for me and my children, which is why I believe God caused the eviction to happen suddenly. I probably would not have left if I wasn't evicted.

The next day, we moved out and went to stay at Extended Stay America. It cost close to $1,500 a month to live there, and I had an income of $1,200 at that time. To keep the anxiety down, I told myself that we would take it one day at a time. Within two weeks of staying there, I was out of money. My bank account was in the negative, and when I went to swipe my card to pay for our stay for the next week, the transaction was declined. *OMG! What am I going to do?* Panic began to set in; I broke down and started to cry. The only thing that kept going through my mind was that my children and I were going to have to sleep in the car until I could get some more money. I called local shelters in the area to check availability, but they were all booked. I reached out to family and some friends, and some told me no; others gave me reasons why they had no room in their homes, and I also heard, "Your kids can come, but you can't."

The night before we left Extended Stay America, I was online and stumbled upon an article written by Kenneth Hagin titled "The Believer's Authority Regarding Finances," and I came across a prayer he said he prayed when he was starting his ministry and depending on God to meet his weekly needs of $150. He said he prayed, "In Jesus' Name, I claim one hundred and fifty dollars this week. Satan, take your hands off my money in Jesus' Name." Then I also said, "Go, ministering spirits, and cause the money to come." I wondered to myself if the prayer would really work if I prayed and asked God for $3,000 because that's how much I needed to pay rent and get my car fixed. As I began to say the prayer, I found myself *not wanting to be greedy*, and instead of asking for $3,000, I prayed for $1,000. I said the prayer twice just in case it didn't go through the first time.

The next day, I forgot all about the prayer when we found ourselves sitting at McDonald's restaurant, trying to figure out where to go for the night. As midnight hit, we drove to a Walmart parking lot, and with our blankets in hand, my children and I tried to sleep in our car. I couldn't get comfortable and kept opening my eyes, wondering if someone was going to rob us. I got up and said, "We're going down the street to this other hotel," and I was going to swipe my card and pray for it to go through, and that's what exactly happened. That night, we ended up staying in that hotel. Thank You, God, for day 1. The next day, I had my oldest son stay home to watch the children while I went out and drove for Lyft to make some money to cover that night. Everything went as planned, and upon coming home, I paid for us to stay another night, day 2.

The next day, everything seemed to be going fine until I went to my second son's school to pick him up and saw my mother, the one who evicted us from our home, sitting and talking with the principal in her office. Anger went through my body, and before I knew it, I felt myself getting worked up on the inside. I sat down in the office and asked them why she was there when I had specifically taken her name off the list of people who could pick my child up from school. I was told that she was worried about her grandchildren because we were homeless, and she wanted to see my son Jaylen. I sat there, thinking to myself, *Why is she really here?* My mother is a narcissistic, and if you know anything about narcissistic mothers, they love to provoke a response from you. So, I got up and wrote the principal a note to give me a call when she's done speaking with my mother, and then I left. I was upset the entire day and just told myself to not pay her any attention.

The next day, which was day 3, a Friday, my mother began to call my phone over and over, and then she texted me: "You have a check here for $4,000." I thought to myself, *Yeah, right! You're just trying to get me to come back over there because you know you were wrong.* Then my grandmother called me and said, "Taquila, you better stop acting crazy and get over there to your mother's house; she has a check for you." Maybe she's not lying, so I headed to my mom's house, and to my surprise, she handed me an envelope from the IRS with a check of $3,650 inside. Do you remember the prayer I prayed? How much was I going to ask God for before changing my mind? $3,000! That night, I experienced the love of God. One of my love languages is acts of services. So, when you do something for me—help me out and show me you have my back—I feel loved by you, and that night, I felt loved by God. That night, God let me know that I was not alone; He was there with me, always has my back, and will not only protect me but also provide for me and His grandchildren—just like a loving father is supposed to. This is the kind of encounter you need in order for you to know that God is real. God loves you and is with you. This kind of encounter with God is what heals the orphan spirit.

CHAPTER 3
BREAK FREE FROM THE SPIRIT
OF DEPRESSION

I was asked the question: "How do I stop feeling depressed when I think about the future of my baby and I?" I completely understand this question, and in fact, this was where I was back in 2014 when I found myself pregnant with my third baby. I had no job, no saving, and I was in debt, little to no money coming in to support my then two children, and I was having problems with my car. My future looked completely hopeless, and on top of everything, I kept finding myself consumed with depression and obsessing over why he left and if he was going to come back. I really wanted my daughter to have her father in her life and not grow up having to experience what it's like to be rejected by one's own father. For this reason, I had a hard time understanding why he was so cold-hearted and wanted nothing to do with me or the baby.

Why is he so cold-hearted?

Cold-hearted: lacking affection or warmth; unfeeling.

Synonyms: unfeeling, unloving, uncaring, unemotional, unkind, insensitive, indifferent, detached, hard-hearted, stony-hearted, with a heart of stone, heartless, hard, harsh, cold.

Romans 1:28–32 (NIV): "Furthermore, since they did not think it worthwhile to retain the knowledge of God, *he gave them over to a **depraved mind***, to do what ought not to be done. They have become filled with every kind of wickedness, evil, greed and depravity. They are full of envy, murder, strife, deceit and malice. They are gossips, slanderers, God-haters, insolent, arrogant and boastful; they invent ways of doing evil; they disobey their parents; they are senseless, faithless, ***heartless***, ruthless. Although they know God's righteous decree that those who do such things deserve death, they not only continue to do these very things but also approve of those who practice them."

He's cold-hearted because God gave him over to a depraved mind. A depraved mind comes from refusing to acknowledge God and choosing to live how you want to live and making up your own rules. I remember when I was pregnant with my daughter; I was talking to him over the phone, and he was trying to convince me to have an abortion. He mentioned how he told one of the ladies he counseled in his program to have an abortion because the father didn't want the baby, and she was already having financial problems. Thus, he placed the seed in her mind to have an abortion and get rid of him too, and her problems would be solved. I remember saying to him that he shouldn't tell women to abort their children, even if they come asking for help concerning their situation. I quickly reminded him of the church we both came from and what we know to be true concerning the Word of God, which is: God is against abortion. I told him he was wrong for telling her that and that she was still going to continue to have problems even after she had the abortion, and he was quiet over the phone. I honestly believe the Holy Spirit was speaking through me in that moment because I had never corrected someone like that in my life before; this is a prime example of having a depraved mind. In his mind, even though he knew what the Word of God says, he went against it and shared what he thought was best for her situation.

Now, here's the part you must understand when it pertains to your baby's father: if he's cold-hearted toward you and his unborn child, then you must recognize that God has given him over to his own fleshly desires, which is designed to cause him to destroy himself. So, trying to convince him as to why he needs to be a part of your child's life is a waste of time. The only thing that will change his mind is God, but not without repentance and turning away from his sinful ways. So, find closure in knowing that it was nothing you did that caused him to act cold toward you. When you reflect over the relationship, you may discover some of his deceitful and wicked ways. In the meantime, what you can do on behalf of your child's father is, begin to pray and intercede for him. Pray that God may have mercy on his soul. Pray that the scales come off his eyes and ears and that he turns from his wicked ways and sees where he has fallen short and repents before God. Pray that God restores his soul, creates in him a clean heart, and renews a right spirit within him in Jesus' name.

Is it God's Will for You to Be Alone?

I don't believe it's God's will for you to be alone, raising your child all by yourself. In Genesis, the first chapter, when God created Adam and Eve, He gave them the instruction to be fruitful and increase in number; fill the earth and subdue it. This lets you know that God had family in mind from the very beginning. Psalm 27:10 says, "Though my father and mother forsake me, the Lord will receive me." But why is that? I believe it's because God does not want His children roaming around the earth without a Father because that would contradict His Word in John 14:18, which says, "I will not leave you as orphans; I will come to you." We also see the angel of the Lord going after Hagar in Genesis 16 when she fled from Sarai because she was being maltreated while pregnant with Abram's child. Verse 7 says, "The angel of the Lord found Hagar near a spring in the desert; it was the spring that is beside the road to Shur, And he said, 'Hagar, servant of Sarai, where have you come from, and where are you going?' 'I'm running away from my mistress Sarai', she answered. Then the angel of the Lord told her, 'Go back to your mistress and submit to her.' The angel added, 'I will so increase your descendants that they will be too numerous to count.'"

Now you're probably wondering, *Why would God send His angel to tell Hagar to go back when Sarai was mistreating her?* I believe it was because she was pregnant with Abram's child, and even though Abram and Sarai went out of the will of God by trying to build their family through another woman, Abram was still held responsible for the baby that was in Hagar's womb. And you also see that God still turned their mess around for good by telling Hagar, "I will so increase your descendants that they will be too numerous to count." This restored hope back unto Hagar and let her know that God never forgot about her. So, I don't believe God would cause your baby's father to leave you while pregnant so that you can be a single mother raising your baby all on your own. God is a God of order, and Him causing the father to abandon you is out of order. Now, however, I do believe that God can turn around the mess we got ourselves in for our good. If you are sensing God telling you to let go of your baby's father, He's telling you this for a reason. God could be trying to work on your relationship right now so that He could not only purge a few things out from within you but also heal your wounds, and your baby's father being in the picture right now could become a distraction for you and vice versa.

God knows what's going on inside of your baby's father's heart, and He also knows how stubborn men can be. So, He has to take your child's father through a couple of trials, errors, and hardships to get him back on track and do right by you and his child. So, it is not over for you. God has to get both of you back on track and in right standing with Him so that you can raise your child on a foundation that's built on the Lord.

"But My Mother Was a Single Mother Raising Her Children Alone, and Now I'm Alone."

What you are referring to is what has caused generational curses. Generational curses are when we observe, as children, our mothers, as single mothers, struggling to keep food on the table and making poor choices in men, and we find ourselves as adults choosing the same kind of men our mothers dated, who would lie, cheat, and get you pregnant, only to leave you with a child, and you, too, find yourself struggling to raise your kids. You just repeated what you saw your mother go through. So, just because your mother was a single mother, and now you're a single mother, doesn't mean you must be alone for the rest of your life. No! What this means is, you must now become the bloodline breaker and break this curse off your family bloodline so that your daughter doesn't repeat it.

"How did this ever become a curse in my family bloodline?"

I'm glad you asked. In the book of Deuteronomy 28, you will find blessings for obedience and curses for disobedience. This particular curse could have come somewhere in your mother's bloodline that she's not aware of, and it just continues from generation to generation. Also, the curse could have come in through disobedience and sin. Deuteronomy 5:8–9 says, "You shall not make for yourself an idol in the form of anything in heaven or on the earth beneath or in the waters below. You shall not bow down to them or worship them; for I, the Lord your God, am a jealous God, punishing the children for the sin of the fathers to the third and fourth generation of those who hate me."

Now, here's what God revealed to me after the breakup with my daughter's father and how I made him become an idol in my life. After he left, I immediately began to panic; I was terrified at the thought of not being able to raise my children on my own because I was already struggling as a single mom. So, I began to look to him to come back and save me, and we get married, and he buys me a house and pays all the bills. God also brought back to my mind how, before getting pregnant, I would look to my daughter's father for all the answers in my life instead of seeking God. So, I had to repent and ask God for forgiveness for making him an idol in my life.

If my story sounds familiar to you, I suggest you repent and ask God for forgiveness as well. **Remember this:** The curses are tied to the choices we make. When you choose to abort your child because your boyfriend asked you to, you bring yourself up under a curse. When you choose to give in to him and have sex with him because you fear he's going to leave, you bring yourself under a curse. When you choose to mess around with him, even though he's married but separated, both of you are under a curse. Deuteronomy 28:18 says, "The fruit of your womb will be cursed," and I believe one of the ways this curse comes about is when fathers are missing from the home.

How do you break generational curses?

1. Pray and ask God to forgive you and your family for causing this curse to come upon your family bloodline. Ask God to forgive you and your family for operating in sin, worshipping idols, for not keeping the Lord's commandments, and any other thing you can think of that opened the door for this curse to come into your bloodline. Ask God to break the curse going back all the way to Adam in Jesus' name. Begin to declare the blessings of God (Deut 28:1–14) in your life now in Jesus' name.

2. Renew your mind with the Word of God. Begin to read your Bible so that it can remove any belief that is not in alignment with the Word of God.

3. Make better choices. Choose to live right and be in right standing with God. Whatever area of your life that you find yourself falling into sin, begin to ask God to teach you how to overcome and to help you make the right choice so that you don't find yourself falling into sin all over again.

Know Who You Are in Christ

1 Peter 2:9 reveals to us who we are in Christ: "But you are a chosen people, a royal priesthood, a holy nation, a people belonging to God."

"But you are a chosen people ..." I want you to replace the word 'people' with 'daughter' and then read it again: "But you are a chosen daughter." Repeat after me: "I am chosen by God."

"A royal priesthood"

Royal - having the status of a king or queen or a member of their family.

Priesthood - the office or position of a priest.

Repeat after me: "I am a queen. I am a part of God's family."

"A holy nation"

Repeat: "I am holy."

"A people belonging to God"

Repeat: "I belong. I belong to God. I have a home."

Here is your foundation of who God says you are: You are not who you think you are. You are not a mistake. You are not who he said you are. You are not what your family calls you. You are a child of God.

This verse is what changed my life and helped me come into my true identity in Christ. *Depression cannot reside in a person who knows who they are.* The minute God revealed to me my identity in Christ, depression began to break off me. When you're depressed, you feel worthless, like there's no use for you, but I'm here to tell you that the reason why the devil is fighting you so hard is that he knows who you are, and he's afraid that once you get the revelation of who you are in Christ, you are going to do damage to his kingdom. You are not who you think you are. You are not just a mother. You are not what you do (your career/job). You are who God says you are, and you are what God called you to do.

Who does God say you are?

- You are a son

- You are a child of God

- You are the light of this world (Matthew 5:14)

- You are the apple of God's eye (Zechariah 2:8)

- You are precious and honored in God's sight (Isaiah 43:4)

- You are fearfully and wonderfully made (Psalm 139:14)

- You are holy and dearly loved; full of compassion, kindness, humility, gentleness, and patience (Colossians 3:12)

- You are forgiven (Colossians 1:13–14)

- You are love

- You are loved by God

- You are a new creature (2 Corinthians 5:17)

- You are justified (Romans 5:1)

- You are an heir of God and a co-heir with Christ (Romans 8:17)

- You are the head and not the tail (Deut. 28:13)

- You will lend to many nations but will borrow from none (Deut.28:12)

- You are healed (1 Peter 2:24)

- You are more than a conqueror (winner, victor, champion, defeater) (Romans 8:37)

- You are chosen (Ephesians 1:4)

- You are peace (Philippians 2:5)

- Your body is a temple of the Holy Spirit (1 Corinthians 6:19)

- You have a spirit of power, of love, and of self-discipline (2 Timothy 1:7)

As you read the Bible, continue to find scriptures of who God says you are and say them out loud each day. You can also type into Google "Scriptures on Identity" and start there.

What is it that God called you to do?

Jeremiah 29:11 says, "For I know the plans I have for you, declares the Lord, plans to prosper you and not to harm you, plans to give you hope and a future." God created you to solve a specific problem, and it is up to you to discover the calling on your life. To help you get started, go to https://gifts.churchgrowth.org/spiritual-gifts-survey/gifts-survey/ and take the spiritual gift assessment to discover your top three dominant gifts which will help you to understand your personality type, why you're drawn to certain things, and what it means for your life. My top three spiritual gifts are Mercy, Shepherding, and Serving.

People always tell me that they love talking to me—and I'm a great listener as they pour out their deepest hurts and pain to me. I often hear them say, "I don't know why I'm telling you this," but I know why, and it's because this is what God called me to do—to provide comfort and counsel people, letting them know they are not alone, the gift of Mercy. The gift of Shepherding is what I'm doing right now with this book; I'm teaching you how to navigate this season of depression and pregnancy on your own. Now, this gift came as a shock to me because, even though I always felt led to help women, I was hesitant to put myself out there and share my story of being abandoned not once but twice while pregnant. I looked at it as embarrassing, but God began to reveal to me that there are more women just like me going through this same thing and are need of help, healing, and guidance.

The gift of serving/service comes into play when women reach out to me at one o'clock in the morning sad and needing someone to talk to, and I spend an hour of my time listening, guiding, and instructing them on what to do in order to get to a place of healing. I always hear "Thanks for taking the time to talk to me" because other people they reached out to either ignored them or took their sweet time getting back to them. People with the service gift have the desire and patience to walk with anyone that's hurting or find themselves in distress. So, your homework is to go to the link above and take the assessment test to discover your top three spiritual gifts.

Who are you?

Once you've discovered who God says you are, and your top three spiritual gifts, then you want to bring it all together and write down who you are. Here's a list of who I am:

- I am a counselor

- I am a healer

- I am a teacher

- I am a leader

- I am authoritative (reliable, trustworthy, true, dependable, respected, self-confident, self-assured, confident)

- I am expressive

- I am composed

- I am sensitive

- I am a good listener

- I am peaceable

- I am agreeable

- I am outgoing

- I am love

- I feel with others

- I am easy to talk to

- I say the right thing at the right time

- I have an inoffensive personality

- I am merciful

- I am a servant

- I am a shepherd

- I identify with people

- I work well with abused women

- I am responsive to people

- I am faithful

- I am loyal

- I am devoted

- I am relationship oriented

- I am sincere

- I am likable

- I am tolerant

- I am a child of God

- I am the apple of God's eye

- I am valuable

- I am set apart

- I am called for such a time as this

- I am the head and not the tail, above and not beneath

What did Jesus say about himself? "I am the way." "I am the truth and the light." "I am the son of God." "I am a healer." "I am able." Jesus knew who He was, and He confessed it everywhere He went. Who are you? When you find out who you are and what you're called to do, then you will find where your money is at. "A man's gift maketh room for him, and bringeth him before great men" (Proverbs 18:16, *KJV*).

CHAPTER 4
HOW TO HEAL FROM A
BROKEN HEART

"He heals the brokenhearted and binds up their wound." –
Psalm 147:3

In this section, I want to take you through the inner healing process and help you recover after the breakup. Healing comes from God. So, as you go through this process, I want you to keep yourself in the presence of God because that's where you will find healing and restoration. You can fast, pray, turn on worship music and allow it to play in the background as you work through the material and also read the Bible.

Delete and Block

If you were to hire a personal trainer to help you lose weight— 20 pounds, to be exact—the first thing he would do is put you on some kind of fast or cleanse for the first one to 10 days to help jumpstart your weight loss. The goal is to give your body a break from all of the unhealthy toxic foods it's used to getting in order to cleanse itself, and you lose weight of five pounds of water in the process. This is the same thing you must do when starting your healing process. You must take time away from the thing that's hurting your heart and purge yourself from its toxicity so that your heart can start to heal back to wholeness again.

The first step in this process is to delete your ex's number from your phone so that when the urge to call him comes, his number is already deleted from your phone. Remember, he walked away from you while pregnant, so he needs to be calling and coming back to you, not you constantly calling and/or texting him emotional messages. If it makes you feel better, you can write his number down in your phone book since he is the father of your child, and you need to call him one day concerning the baby, but for now, take his phone number out of your phone. Unfriend him on social media and then block him. Again, this stops you and him from looking at one another's pages, trying to see what's new in each other's life. Now, I'm well aware of the fact that you can simply unblock him, but when you go to your settings to unblock his name, that's enough time for you to really think if looking at his page is something you really want to do.

Next, get rid of all the memories of him. Get rid of all the pictures you two took of each other. Get rid of old love letters, cards, gifts he's gotten you for your birthday or holiday, any piece of furniture that reminds you of him; the lingerie you used to wear for him, get rid of it. Stop listening to love songs that cause you to feel sorry about yourself and wish he was still there. You have to get ridiculous crazy with getting rid of everything that reminds you of him. Memories are triggers. So, as you are going through this process of healing, you don't want to be going strong for 90 days and then stumble upon an old picture of the two of you, which then causes you to start thinking about him, and before you know it, you're calling him up, and he's at your house and in your bed again. This is why you must get rid of all the memories now so that nothing throws you off track later on down the line.

The Grieving Process

When a relationship ends suddenly, you will immediately go through a grieving process where you will begin to experience different emotions such as anger, depression, sadness, and sometimes happiness—then back to resenting him and wanting revenge. One day, you would tell yourself to forget all about him, only for you to wake up the next day crying, wishing he was still here with you. Depression will hit you hard, having you feel unloved, rejected, wondering why he doesn't care about you, and feeling hopeless about your situation. Find closure in knowing that you're not losing your mind. You're not crazy; you are experiencing what is called the five stages of grief. The five stages of grief are denial, anger, bargaining, depression, and acceptance. In no particular order, you will experience these things.

I lived in the denial stage for close to two years until I went for counseling and got additional help to move me out of that stage. As you go through this process, allow yourself to go through each emotion and stage of the grieving process, but don't get stuck there. If years have passed, and you're finding it hard to accept he's moved on, you may need to seek out professional help such as seeing a therapist help you work through why you're having a hard time accepting the fact that he's moved on and why you should too. One thing that will help you in this process is writing down what you are feeling inside and releasing your emotions. Being abandoned by someone you love will cause feelings of anger and revenge to creep up in you. So, to help you not act on these emotions, you want to find healthy ways to get them off you so you don't walk around feeling angry, depressed, and taken advantage of. Here are some questions to help you get started in releasing your emotions:

1. How did his leaving make you feel?

2. How did it make you feel when he asked you to have an abortion?

3. What is it that you're having a hard time wrapping your brain around?

4. What are you feeling confused about?

5. What words did he say to you that still goes through your mind?

6. What are you angry about?

7. What are you disappointed about?

8. Do you want revenge?

9. If you were to act on the revenge, would it help this situation?

10. How do you feel about yourself after all of this?

11. What are you afraid of?

12. What are you having a hard time accepting?

13. If you were to let him go, what would this represent in your life?

14. What do you need him to give you closure regarding?

The Forgiveness Process

I'm sure you've heard the saying that forgiveness is for you, not the person who hurt you. Forgiveness is a decision you make concerning the other person, where you decide, "I will no longer be upset about what happened in this situation; I'm no longer walking around filled with anger and bitterness but making the decision to let it go and move on." When you forgive, that doesn't mean you forget what they did to you. Forgiving your child's father for turning his back on you and his child does not make you appear weak; it doesn't let him off the hook either. No! The Bible tells us, "Do not be deceived, a man reaps what he sows," and God sees everything done to you, and in due time, you will be vindicated, but until then, you must forgive. When you hold onto unforgiveness, it blocks you from receiving healing. Unforgiveness blocks your money from flowing into your life. Unforgiveness keeps you stuck in the past, unable to move forward. Unforgiveness opens the door to satan to come in, attack your mind, and torment you with thoughts of him not caring about you, how everyone did you wrong, causing you to feel sorry for yourself, which also causes you to go deeper into depression to the point you might consider suicide, thinking life would be much better if you weren't here. When you don't forgive, you miss the blessing of God, and it also causes you to not enjoy being pregnant but dread it and can't wait until it's over. So, put an end to the devil's scheme by choosing to forgive your ex and welcome healing.

Complete the following sentence:

I forgive you (say your ex's name) for

_____

_____

_____

_____

_____

_____

_____

_____

_____

_____

I let go of

_____

_____

_____

_____

_____

_____

_____

_____

_____

_____

I ask You, Lord, to come into my heart, my mind, and my soul and heal every wound that resulted from the breakup with my baby's father.

Allow yourself to dwell in God's presence as He begins to heal you from the inside out. As you go through this forgiveness process, you may feel yourself wanting to cry, but I want to encourage you to allow the tears to flow because that's pent-up anger inside of you coming out. If at any time you get to the point where you feel like hurting yourself or someone else, stop and seek help immediately. Do not act on your feelings.

Next, after going through this process, you want to forgive yourself for holding on to all of this anger, for giving him a chance to hurt you, for choosing a deadbeat to be the father of your child, etc.

I forgive myself for:

_____

_____

_____

_____

_____

_____

_____

_____

_____

_____

Break The Soul Tie

If you find yourself constantly thinking about him and can't seem to get him out of your mind, then what you have is a strong soul tie with your ex that needs to be broken. To help you get a better understanding of what a soul tie is and how they are formed, let's take a closer look at the word 'soul tie.'

Your soul is your mind, your will, the place where you make a decision from, and your emotions. When you have formed a soul tie with a person, you find yourself constantly thinking about them (your mind). You tend to be up and down in your emotions, and even though they hurt you, and you tell yourself "I'm done. I'm not giving him a second chance," when he comes back, you find yourself giving in to him and having sex with him all over again, only for him to hurt you like before, and you are left wondering why you can't just be strong and let him go. It's not that you can't be strong; it's the soul tie that needs breaking because it now has affected your will (the place where you make decisions from), and when it's broken, you tend to not see things clearly and not make unwise decisions, e.g., having sex with him again, only for him to disappear again.

How are soul ties formed? Unhealthy soul ties are formed when we engage in sex outside of marriage with a person who is not our husband. You then form a spiritual tie where both of your souls are connected in the spirit. This is why you find yourself constantly thinking about him; he's showing up in your dreams; you begin to act and even sound like him and have a hard time moving on.

How to break soul ties: To break the soul ties formed with your baby's father, say the following prayer: "Heavenly Father, I ask that You forgive me for entering into the relationship with (say his name) and forming an unhealthy soul tie. I ask that You break any and all soul ties that were formed knowingly and unknowingly in Jesus' name. I come out of agreement with any word connection that's keeping him and I connected in the spirit such as 'He is my husband, and I am his wife.' I ask that You break the word connection with the sword of the spirit in Jesus' name."

After you break the soul tie, next, you want to ask God to restore your soul. Psalm 147:3 says, "He heals the brokenhearted and binds up their wounds." The word 'heart' also refers to your mind. So, when you begin to pray and ask God to restore your soul, He's going to not only restore and heal your heart but also restore your mind, will, and emotions back to its original condition.

Restore: return something or someone to its former condition.

In the presence of God, you find restoration. What this means is, you have to get before God in fasting, prayer, praise, and worship and allow the presence of God to saturate your entire body. Turn on some worship music and begin to call out God's many names:

- Jehovah Jireh, my provider

- Jehovah Rapha, the Lord who heals me

- Jehovah Nissi, the Lord my banner

- Jehovah Shalom, the Lord my peace

- Elohim - Mighty One

- Alpha and Omega

- The beginning and the end

- You reign with all power and authority on heaven and earth

- You are mercy

- You are awesome

- You are mighty in battle

- You are the Prince of Peace

- You are a good Father

- I praise Your Holy name.

You want to go into full praise and worship to God. Then begin to thank God for all He's done in your life. After thanksgiving, ask God to restore your soul back to its original condition.

The Word of God is another way through which we can receive restoration. My testimony is, God healed my heart in 30 days and delivered me from depression with one Scripture, 1 Corinthians 8:1, "Love builds up." At the time, I felt stuck, unable to move forward. I asked God, "How do I get over him?" God led me to 1 Corinthians 8:1, and as I continued reading the following scriptures, my eyes kept going back to reread what it said:

-Love builds up ... If love builds up, then why is he tearing me down, pointing out my flaws, causing me to feel bad about myself?

-Love builds up ... If love builds up, then why did he stop caring about me and talking to me once I got pregnant?

If love builds up, then why do the people who say they love me act like they don't? Why is my family constantly tearing me down and talking bad about me?

Hebrews 4:12–13 (NIV), "For the word of God is living and active. Sharper than any double-edged sword, it penetrates even to dividing soul and spirit, joints and marrow; it judges the thoughts and attitudes of the heart. Nothing in all creation is hidden from God's sight. Everything is uncovered and laid bare before the eyes of him to whom we must give account."

When the Word of God gets on the inside of you, it exposes the lies you currently believe and breaks you free in the process. There's the part of you that still loves him after all he put you through, and you're wondering if he really loved you. Well, let's take a look at the true meaning of love.

Where does love come from? According to 1 John 4:7, love comes from God, and we see that in 1 John 4:16, God is love. This is your foundation of love.

Now let's take a look at your current foundation of love. Answer the questions below:

1. What were you taughts about love?

2. How did your mother express her love for you?

3. How did your father express his love for you?

4. How do the people who love you treat you?

5. How do these same people speak to you? Do they call you names? Do they put you down and cause you to feel bad about yourself? Do they get mad when you try to improve yourself?

6. How have past boyfriends expressed their love toward you? Did they cheat on you, verbally abuse you, use and mistreat you? Were you always breaking up to make up?

When you begin to answer these questions, you will discover your current love language and why you're in love with a man who abandoned you and your unborn baby. Your current love language is not the true meaning of love but *toxic love*, an unhealthy way of loving you were taught by your family and friends.

How do you know the love you have with him is toxic? Because his love is based on conditions. "I'll love you, and we'll continue to be together if you get an abortion." When it's true love, it comes with no condition—he continues to love you even if you get pregnant. He sticks around to take care of his child. Your true love takes responsibility for his action and would man up instead of placing blame onto the woman, saying such things as "You're ruining my life" or "You did this on purpose." True love works through whatever problems exist. When it's true love, you are protected from harm and cared for, no matter what. True love does not watch you suffer and struggle; it helps you out. Your homework in this section is to allow God to give you a better love language by teaching you the true meaning of love. Read and meditate on the Scriptures below:

Love comes from God (1 John 4:7)

God is love (1 John 4:16)

Love builds up (1 Corinthians 8:1)

Love is patient and kind (1 Corinthians 13:4)

Love never fails (1 Corinthians 13:8)

Love rebukes and disciplines (Revelations 3:19)

His love endures forever (2 Ch 5:13)

"Praise be to God, who has not rejected my prayer or **withheld** his love from me!" (Psalm 66:20). (*Withhold: refuse to give something that is desired by another; suppress or hold back an emotion or reaction.*)

Love must be **sincere** (Romans 12:9). (*Sincere: free from pretense or deceit.*) Love is honest, truthful, genuine, real, and upfront

Love does no **harm** to its neighbor (Romans 13:10).

(*Harm: injury, hurt, wound, mistreat, misuse, abuse, torment, pain, suffering, distress, trauma, damage, ruin, molest, inflict pain on, handle/treat roughly, do violence to, destroy.*)

Love does not delight in evil (1 Corinthian 13:6).

Being rooted and established in love (Ephesians 3:17).

Speaking the truth in love (Ephesians 4:15).

Whoever does not love does not know God because God is love (1 John 4:8).

CHAPTER 5
HOW DO I COPE WITH HIM MOVING ON?

"You know you're healed when your baby daddy is no longer your type." ~ Taquila Coleman

The way you cope with him moving on to another woman is by continuing to do your own inner healing work and becoming a better woman in the process. When you are healed and understand your worth and value, and you know that you deserve better than what he is currently offering you, you no longer care about what he is or isn't doing or who he's with.

The reason why you find yourself constantly checking up on him, checking his social media page, is that you feel forgotten, you feel less than, and you're wondering why he chose her over you—as if something is wrong with you. My goal for you in this section is to help you to identify and see your own worth and value so that you're no longer waiting around for a man who refuses to see your worth.

I know people probably have told you that you deserve better ... but what does that really mean? To *deserve* means to have **earned** something or be given something because of your actions, your behavior, or the qualities you have. To earn something requires effort. When people tell you that you deserve better when it pertains to your baby daddy, what they are saying is, you deserve better treatment than he is currently giving you. Since getting pregnant, he left you, stopped calling you, blocked you, refused to come to any of your prenatal visits, acts like you and the baby don't exist. Wouldn't you agree that you deserve better treatment than this? But what do we do when we find ourselves abandoned while pregnant? We continue to reach out to him, try to act nice when he does finally decide to talk to us; we end up sleeping with him again, only for him to hurt us all over again. And we do all of these things when he hasn't earned it or put any effort into the relationship. Let's change this! From this moment on, if he's not putting any effort into you or being apart of the baby's life, then you put no effort into him. See, men respect standards, and in order for him to begin to act right and take you seriously, you have to develop respect for yourself and then teach him how to treat you.

Respect shows people the way you want them to treat you. So, the first thing I want you to do is, write down how your baby's father makes you feel disrespected, and then write next to it how you will respond the next time he decides to disrespect you. The last time I saw my daughter's father in person, he was talking to me about the conversation he had with his mother before she passed away. He said something that caught my attention. "I told my mother about my secret," he said. "What is your secret?" I asked. He responded, "Miracle," referring to my daughter. Now, because I wanted to hear exactly what he told his mother and how that conversation went, I didn't correct him about referring to my daughter as a 'secret.'

Once home, I immediately came up with how I was going to respond the next time he called my daughter a secret. Now, here's the thing: he may not see it as disrespectful, but I do because, for one, she has a name, which is Miracle, and two, if he doesn't feel comfortable referring to her as his daughter, then he should simply call her by her name. This is exactly what I mean by identifying the disrespect and preparing yourself to respond the next time the disrespect shows up because it will teach him a few things about you:

1. You now have standards.

2. You no longer tolerate his disrespect.

3. If he wants to continue to see and/or talk with you, he has to meet your standard.

This is how you get a man to see your value. Isaiah 43:4 says, " ... since you are precious and honored in my sight and because I love you." The word *precious* means *of great value; not to be wasted or treated carelessly.* Synonyms for precious are valuable, costly, expensive, high-priced, dear, invaluable, priceless, rare, choice, fine, irreplaceable. Your value is found in God, and here is what He wants you to know:

- You are valuable

- You are to be treated with care, so don't allow anyone to mistreat you, not even yourself

- You are dear to Me (God)

- You are priceless, so don't ever let someone else determine your value and/or the kind of treatment they are going to give you

- You are rare, one of a kind

- You are different

- You are special

- You are exceptional

- You are outstanding and unique

- You are incomparable, so there's no need for competition

- You are fine

- You are excellent

- Carry yourself as first-class

- You are great

- You are admirable

- You have class

- You are a woman of character

- You are magnificent

- You are beautiful

- You are wonderful

- You are top-notch

- You are worthy

- You are a respectable person

- You are attractive and good-looking

- You are irreplaceable

- You are of great value

- And I love you

So, how do you cope with him moving on? It's by becoming a better woman. Take the focus off him and put it on yourself. Start working on improving yourself daily. Read personal development books. Get to know how God sees you down in your spirit so that you start seeing yourself the same way God sees you. Develop a new standard of treatment.

CHAPTER 6
HOW TO HAVE A BABY SHOWER WITHOUT A PARTNER

Are you considering not having a baby shower because you're dreading people judging you and/or asking you questions about the father? When I was pregnant with my second son, I wasn't able to have a baby shower because of my water breaking at 24 weeks' pregnant and being forced to stay in the hospital until I delivered. While in the hospital, I worried every day about what I was going to do and how I was going to get everything for my baby once I delivered him and we went home, but thank God for my mother who came through just in time and bought the bassinet, baby clothes, diapers, wipes, bottles, and other things. Fast forward two years later, I was back in the same position, but this time, I made sure not to be under any unnecessary stress so that I wouldn't go into labor early or risk miscarrying. Even though this pregnancy was a healthy pregnancy, I still found myself dreading having a baby shower because I didn't want people judging me or asking me questions about where the father was, why he's not around, and what happened between him and I. So, I came to the conclusion of not having a baby shower and to buy everything my baby needed on my own.

If my story sounds familiar to you, and you want to have a baby shower but don't want people asking you about the dad and judging you, I will show you three ways to have a baby shower without answering questions about him. You should be enjoying all of the perks that come with being pregnant, such as having a baby shower, receiving gifts, and spending time with loved ones. I'm going to show you exactly how to do it below:

1. You don't have to answer the questions. It never dawned on me that I could still have my baby shower and not talk about the father as long as I set the standard ahead of time. How profound is that? When one of your family members asks, "Where's the father?" you could simply respond by saying, "I'm sorry, but we're not discussing the father. I would like for us all to focus on our new addition to the family and enjoy one another's time today." This is your baby shower, and if you don't want to discuss or answer any questions about the father, don't!

2. You can also have something small, maybe a dinner with 5–10 people who are supportive and that you can have that kind of experience with without having to answer those questions.

3. You can create a baby shower registry, make the list, and let people know: "I'm so excited about the baby coming. I do have a lot going on right now, so I'm not going to have a baby shower, but if you would like to buy me something, here is the baby list." Come up with a least of 15–20 people and let them know about it.

CHAPTER 7
WHY HE SHOULD PAY CHILD SUPPORT

In this section, I want to talk to you about why you should put him on child support, and why he needs to pay. Now, I understand that there are some women who prefer not to put their baby daddy on child support, with excuses such as "I'm not going through all of that" or "He knows he has a child; if he wants to take care of it, then he will, but I'm not about to force him."

It's not about forcing him to take care of his child but helping him to fill the role he was created for. The role of a father is to give identity to his wife and children (by taking on his last name), establish a vision, create direction, and rule in the home. He is to provide protection, shelter, clothing, food, guidance, care, security, and encouragement. He is to teach and raise his children up in the Lord. A father is to profess his love for his children and take time to bond and connect emotionally with them.

When a man gets you pregnant, decides that he does not want to be a father to that child, and tells you he's not going to help you or pay for the child you're bringing into this world, and you agree with him by not putting him on child support, he is now being taken out of his role as a father. It does not matter that he had no plans on being with the woman long term. He should never have approached and pursued you. He knew, just like you know, that if you have sex, there's a possibility of you getting pregnant and him becoming a father. It is not your fault that he didn't know how to practice self-control and discipline. With fatherhood comes accountability. He is accountable to your child.

Yes, he's saying he doesn't want to be a part of the child's life, but when he leaves this world, he will have to give an account to God of each child he refused to care for. Psalm 27:10 says, "When your mother and father forsake you, the Lord will receive you." The word 'forsake' means 'abandon.' So, what God is saying here is, when the father of your child abandons his child, God steps in and fills the role of Father and begins to make sure you have everything you and your child need. Now, if God steps in to provide for His child, shouldn't he be held accountable to do the same thing too?

What if he's threatening to have your kids taken away if you put him on child support?

You should still put him on child support and deal with his threats later. Here's what you must understand: this man has studied you; he knows your weaknesses, which are your kids, and he's going to say whatever he has to say in order to scare you away from putting him on child support. If he does call CPS on you and says you're unfit and neglect the kids, all you have to do is welcome them into your home and allow them to see for themselves that your kids are well taken care of. I doubt he will try to take you to court for sole custody because he already doesn't want anything to do with your child, so do you really believe he's actually going to put himself in the position to take full responsibility of this child? Not at all! But in case he does take you to court, he would have to prove to the judge how you're unfit, why he should be granted full custody, and he would need to show proof that he has not only the income to take care of the kids but also the time to be with them. He would need to show his proof of residency and everything else. So, don't worry about his threats. Continue to stand your ground and head to the Friend of the Courts building in your county and file for child support.

Should you try and work out an agreement with the father without involving the courts?

No! Remember, he's a deadbeat, and you can't take a deadbeat at his word. This man pursued you, became the man of your dreams, and allowed you to fall in love with him, only to get you pregnant and abandon you. Now you're considering taking him by his word—by working out a verbal agreement of what he said he's going to do for you and what he will pay you? What if you decide to work something out with him, and everything goes well until month three when he decides he doesn't want to continue to pay and gives you excuses like "Oh, my job cut my hours back, so I'm not going to be able to pay this week, but next week, I should be able to give you something"? Now you're left in a bind, trying to figure out how you are going to pay your rent, buy food, or pay your light bill because you were depending on his child support payment. This man needs to prove himself to you that he's serious about being a part of his child's life and being a consistent father. Until he's proven himself to you, I wouldn't take his word on anything.

CHAPTER 8
HOMELESS & PREGNANT:
HOW TO SURVIVE

In this section, I want to talk to you about how to survive being homeless and pregnant. Even though I wasn't homeless when I was pregnant with any of my children, I quickly found my children and I getting evicted from our home in 2018.

Let's start with your money. The only income I had coming in when I found myself homeless was child support and social security, which equalled $1,000 for the month. Since I already had an eviction on my credit, that made it hard for me to get approved for an apartment. I called local shelters, but all were either booked to maximum or, as one lady stated over the phone, "It's too many of us for them to provide beds for." So, my only option was to stay in a hotel until I figured out my next move. With three kids, I made up my mind that I needed a hotel with a stove in there so I could cook instead of trying to cook from a microwave. So, we stayed at Extended Stay America. Staying there for one month cost $1,500, so I had to figure out how I was going to get an extra $500 per month to pay for us to stay there every month.

Before getting evicted, I was already driving for lyft part time but didn't really like it because it gave me extreme anxiety having strangers in my car, so I found another company called DoorDash, which is a food delivery service, where I could deliver people food to their houses or workplace and get paid.

So, I started driving as a delivery driver. The plan was to take my two sons to school in the morning and then start dashing with my daughter afterward. While out dashing, people would see me and my daughter picking up customers' food, and they would say, "I was wondering if I could bring my kids with me," and I would tell them, "Yes, why not! All you're doing is picking up and delivering food to the customers." I would also share with them exactly how I went about doing this with my daughter.

Note that I didn't know if I could or couldn't bring my daughter with me while dashing. I saw an opportunity that would help me bring in some extra money, and I can have my daughter with me instead of putting her in daycare, and I said "Deal, this is what I'm going to do to help pay for our hotel fee every month." If you would like to learn more about how you can make money with doordash without putting your kids in daycare, go to my YouTube channel "Taquila Coleman," subscribe, and click at the top where it says 'Playlist' and watch the playlist titled "DoorDash," and you can sign up too from there.

There's another company called 'Shipt' that you can utilize if you're currently homeless and in need of some extra money. Now, with Shipt, instead of delivering food, you are going to either target or Meijer, doing customers' grocery shopping and delivering items to their homes. You get paid every day with Doordash; they have a fast pay option, but with Shipt, you get paid on a Friday, and it goes directly into your bank account. Shipt has some pros and cons, though. To learn more about it, you can watch the playlist on my channel titled "Shipt" and sign up from there too.

If you enjoy babysitting or love being a Nanny, there's a site called www.care.com where you can go and list babysitting and nanny services. In 2015, I hired my first nanny from that site and ended up keeping her for seven days, and she made $1,000. How would you like to make $1,000 in seven days? Now, a few things to keep in mind about why I chose to hire her:

1. She stood out from the other nannies on that site by recording a 2-minute introduction video of herself.

2. She was available at last minute. I needed her to come to my house the next morning at 6 a.m., and she did.

3. She met all of my needs. I needed a nanny to provide care in my home, take my oldest son to school and pick him up, and then come back home and cook for my children.

4. She was down to earth and likable. Before hiring her we exchanged phone numbers and immediately starting texting one another and getting to know each other.

Another way that will help you pay for your hotel fees is by filling out an application to work at the current hotel you're staying at. This is something else I did at Extended Stay America, except I applied to work at a different location because I didn't want to work where I stayed at too. I get bored quickly, and the people you work with tend to be messy, so I didn't want any of that to cause me to dread living there.

Here are a couple of things you want to keep in mind when living at a hotel:

1. If you're staying for more than 30 days, sign up online as a member so that you can receive the perks and discounts for members who stay longer than 30 days. The regular room rate for one night in Extended Stay America is $100, but because I'm a member and am staying longer than 30 days, my rate dropped all the way down to between $50–$60 per night, which saved me a lot of money when you look at all of what I was getting in my room.

2. Get a storage unit if needed or buy you some storage containers and store your stuff in the closet of your room, under the table, and in the corner.

3. If you're staying in a room where you only have a microwave, consider investing in a crock pot to cook your meals.

4. Get to know the workers at the hotel. One time, I got myself in a bind where I ended up missing four days of payment. One of the ladies asked me when was I going to make another payment because the management was starting to ask questions, so I paid up to date for the days we had stayed and was able to get back on track. Her response to me was, "We didn't bother you because we know you're going to pay, plus you have those kids too." So, I was happy that I took the time to get to know them and have that situation work out in my favor.

5. Take advantage of the free breakfast time. There were times I told my children they better get up and go get

breakfast to eat, or they would have to wait until dinner time to eat because funds were tight then.

6. Use the exercise room to release stress.

7. Don't be afraid to ask questions. Extended Stay America's long-term stay is set up in such a way that you can pay by the week, but there were times when I just didn't have it. So, I asked the manager if I could make a payment every day until I was able to pay by the weeks again, and the answer was yes. Don't be afraid to speak up and ask them if they could work with you until you get back on track. You never know; the answer just might be yes.

CHAPTER 9
SHOULD I CONTACT HIM WHEN
I GO INTO LABOR?

If you are wondering if you should contact him when you go into labor, consider the questions below:

1. Does he know you're pregnant?

2. Does he know how to contact you by phone?

3. Does he know where you live?

If you're nodding your head yes to the questions, then my answer is no! Listen, I understand this is a hurting experience for you, and you want him there in the delivery room cheering you on to have his baby, but that's not the reality of the situation. He already told you what he wants and doesn't want and how he feels about you being pregnant. You must give him time to gather his own thoughts, man up, and do what's right concerning the situation. You have to stop finding *reasons* to contact him because, doing so, you put yourself in the position for further hurt and rejection by him. If he wants to be in the delivery room, he will be there, but if you're at the end of your pregnancy, and he's been missing in action, I wouldn't waste my time trying to call him because he's showing you how he feels about you and the baby—he doesn't care.

If you don't want to be alone in the delivery room, then I would suggest, if you don't have any family or friends supporting you in this pregnancy, to go and join the local single mothers' group in your area. You can also turn to your local church for support.

This is why I suggest single mothers join local single mothers' groups in their area because it opens up the door for you to meet new people and make new mom friends. This also opens up the door for you to build connection and ask for help or support when needed. If you're already a part of a single mothers' group, mention your due date at one of your events and how you might be alone in the delivery room, and they might surprise you in the delivery room by showing up. Also remember, if no one shows up to support you when you go into labor, you always have your doctor and nurse right there supporting you all the way.

CHAPTER 10
SHOULD I TELL HIS FAMILY
ABOUT THE BABY?

"God does not want you to expose him!" Those were the words I heard come out of my pastor's mouth one day while driving in the car. I was hurt, mad, angry, and felt like he was getting away with what he had done to me. It wasn't fair, and I wanted revenge. I knew the best way to go about getting it. First, the idea came to mind to drive down to where he worked with my daughter Miracle strapped in her car seat and then place her right on top of his desk and say in front of everyone in the office, "Meet your daughter!" But my uncle told me not to do that. Then another idea came to mind, *I'm going to expose him when the DNA test comes back*. I had in mind to send each one of his children a copy of the DNA report and a picture of my daughter with the message "Meet your sister!" But once I heard those words come out of my pastor's mouth, I felt convicted inside; I knew God was speaking directly to me. All I could do was ask God: "Why? Why does he get to get away with what he has done?"

I believe the reason why God didn't want me to expose him and doesn't want you to expose your child's father is as follows:

- Just like you are God's child, so is he.

- Exposure causes more hurt and pain in the person who is being exposed.

- "Vengeance is mine," says the Lord.

- God disciplines those He loves. If the father of your child has given his life over to the Lord, then believe that God is going to cause hardship to come upon his life.

- God will give him no rest until he does right by you and his child.

- Exposure interferes with God's plan.

Other things you might want to consider when it comes to exposing the father of your child are:

1. How his side of the family will receive the information and your baby. If he comes from a decent, loving family, they might welcome your baby with open arms and hit him upside the head for trying to keep the baby away. But if his family is not all that welcoming, and you choose to tell them about the baby you have with him, you risk being rejected by his family. Some families are so toxic and unhealthy; they know their son ain't anything, but they stick up for him anyway and encourage his foolishness.

2. How will they treat your child? For this reason, I choose to go the route of allowing the man to be the one who shares the news of his child to his family. Some family members will treat a child they they see the parent treat the child. So, if the father is keeping the baby a secret and already acting like he doesn't care, and you go and tell his family he has a baby with you and start leaving your baby with them, they could possibly start mistreating your child. Even though I'm

not all that close with my father's side of the family, and everyone sees how he doesn't care about being a part of his children's lives, and even though they know he doesn't care, I believe the only reason why they never mistreated my brother and I is that of fear of my mother. My mother would walk into my dad's house, grab a beer bottle, and bust my dad's head in front of all nine of his siblings—brothers and sisters.

3. What if your exposure is what keeps him further away from his child? You never know how God works behind the scene, which is why we must learn how to resist emotions of seeking revenge because the day you decide to expose him could be the day he had made up in his mind to do right by you and his child.

So, to sum it up, I do not encourage exposing him and telling his family about the baby. I believe the father should be the one who tells his own family about his child.

CHAPTER 11
HOW TO TALK TO YOUR CHILD ABOUT THEIR ABSENT FATHER

"**M**om, where's my dad?" This is one question most single mothers dread answering. When my second son was three years old, he took me by surprise by running up to me, asking me where his dad was at. I answered him, "Your dad is in another state." He smiled and said "Okay" and took off running. There's nothing to dread or avoid this question from your child. Simply answer with the truth. I was called a coward by a lady who watched one of my videos on this specific topic where I said to respond to your child with the truth: "Dad is gone because that's what he chose to do." Isn't this the truth? I know in the case of my second son, his father left because he said he had to get himself together, only to later find out he moved out of state and got married. When my son gets older and starts asking more questions about his father, I'm going to tell him the truth. The same thing with my daughter; her father left because he was done raising children and wasn't in the position to help take care of all of my children like he wanted to, so he chose to leave. When my daughter gets to the age where she starts asking about her father, I'm going to sit her down and tell her the truth about why her father chose to not be around.

It's not about lying or making up a story to tell your child as to why their father is not around just to keep from hurting their feelings. What you don't tell your child, somebody else will. If you are not honest with your child about why their father really left, they're going to search the answer out and maybe even go as far as tracking their father down to hear his side of the story, and you already know what he's going to say. If your child comes to you, asking, "Mom, where's daddy?" Tell him or her the truth, and after you tell them, you let them know that you love them and are here for them. When your son gets a certain age, he's going to start to wonder why his brother and sister looks like this person and that person and begin to wonder who he looks like and where he fits in. This is why it's important for you to give him the answers he's looking for because, if not, he's going to turn to the streets for it.

The key to raising boys into men, in my opinion, is identity and purpose. Boys need to know who they are and what they can do. Since his father is missing from the home, it is up to you, Mom, to identify for your son as early as possible what he's good at, his strengths, and guide him in that direction. I already know my middle son is a fixer. He loves to fix things and solve problems, so that's the direction that I'm going to encourage him to go in. My oldest son has an entrepreneurial spirit. He's great at football and basketball and was given the name 'The Playmaker' because of his talent. He's also great with video editing, which I believe is a secondary skillset. My daughter is a natural born leader. Everything she does has influence written on it. So, you find out early on your children's strengths and develop them in those areas. Teach them; learn who they are in Christ.

How to find male mentors for your son when you have no family support or male friends

First, let me encourage you by saying: Don't necessarily assume that because your son's father is missing from your son's life, this will have a negative impact on him. I get compliments all the time on how well respectful my boys are. One guy said to me, "You break your boys in early." What he was referring to was teaching my sons at an early age to take out the trash, how to open a door for a woman, how to meet me at the car and get the grocery bags. I don't take it easy on my sons because their father is not in the home. No! That's not going to help them. I teach my sons how to respect me as their mother, how to respect people in general, how to treat a woman (starting with their sister), how to work to get what they want, how to drive, how to properly care for themselves, and so many other things. I looked at what I wished my parents had done—take the time to teach and show me things instead of just throwing me out to figure out life. Thus, I take time to sit my children down and teach them what they need to know at their current levels.

The way you find a role model and mentor for your son is by identifying the area your son needs mentoring in and finding the mentor that's best suited to help your son in that particular area. If your son shows signs of anger issues early on, then I would recommend you finding him a male therapist to help him get to the root of his anger. If you are looking to help your son develop his confidence and strength, then consider putting him in classes such as Karate or Boxing, where he will be around other boys and male figures that will assist him with building his confidence up. If your son likes to read, you can purchase books for him to read—books that will help to develop him in a particular area. Since all of my children are leaders in their own area of gifting, having them read books by John C. Maxwell on leadership is a great resource to start them off with and then build from there. It doesn't have to be hard trying to find male mentors for your son. Identify the area of mentorship your son needs and find the right person or resources that are best suited for him.

CHAPTER 12
HOW TO ACCEPT THE FACT THAT YOU & YOUR BABY'S FATHER WILL NOT BE TOGETHER LIKE A FAMILY

Are you having a hard time accepting the fact that now you've broken up, you won't have the family you always wanted? And for this reason, you find yourself holding on to him, hard to let go of him because that would mean you will be alone, and that's not what you want. So, what do you do? Get to the root of the real reason why you're having a hard time accepting this in the first place. Your problem is not that you won't have the family you always wanted; your real problem is what you experienced in your own childhood. When you think about how you were raised as a child, what comes to mind? Was your childhood a stable one? Did you have to choose between which parents you wanted to live with? Were there a lot of drama at your mom's house and peace at your dad's house? This is your real problem, what you experienced as a child. Because of what you went through as a child with both of your parents, the back and forth, the unstableness, picking and choosing which side your going to be on in order to make this parent happy, you fear this is what your child will go through if he/she doesn't have both parents together, and for this reason, you continue to hold on to him and refuse to let him go. Here's the good news for you: Your child does not have to experience any of what you experienced in your childhood.

You don't necessarily have to be with the father of your child in order to give your child the family you always wanted. What you must understand is, even though the relationship is over, it doesn't mean you are going to be alone forever. This time next year, you can look up and find yourself married to the man of your dreams, who is ready to take on the role of father and husband and give you the best family you could ever dream of having. But before you can manifest your ideal family, you must first begin to deal with and heal your childhood hurt and pain. Here are ten questions to help you get started with healing childhood trauma as an adult:

1. What was it like living with your mother as a child?

2. What was it like living with your father as a child?

3. How did it make you feel having to go from house to house?

4. How did your dad make you feel as a child?

5. Did your father put other children before you? If yes, how did it make you feel?

6. Did your father place his wife before you? If yes, how did it make you feel?

7. How did your father's side of the family act toward you?

8. How did your mom's side of the family treat you as a child?

9. Did you experience any kind of abuse as a child? If yes, by who? What did this person do to you? How did it make you feel?

10. Make the decision to forgive your mother and father and any other person who mistreated you as a child and let it go! Ask God to come in and heal the wounds of your childhood in Jesus' name.

CHAPTER 13
HOW DO I DEAL WITH THE REJECTION?

You see the breakup as him rejecting you, but what you must understand is that it's not rejection but redirection. The breakup had to happen in order to break you up with your old self. See, the day you prayed to God and asked Him for a husband, a better job, more money, and to reveal your purpose to you, God heard you, and He allowed this breakup to happen so that He could have your full attention in order to speak to you, rebuild you, and course-correct you back in the right direction. The breakup didn't happen to you; it happened for you so that once God brings you out, you can go and share your testimony with the next woman going through this.

Revelation 12:11 (NIV) says, "They overcame him by the blood of the Lamb and by the word of their testimony." It is my testimony of God delivering me from depression and healing my heart that gave you hope to listen to me. Your testimony of how God brought you out and turned a situation that looked completely dead around is going to inspire hope in the next mother going through this same situation.

Ezekiel 37 talks about the valley of dry bones and how the Spirit of the Lord brought Ezekiel out and set him in the middle of a valley full of bones. It says in verse 2, "He led me back and forth among them, and I saw a great many bones on the floor of the valley, bones that were very dry."

Did you know *valley* is a synonym of *depression*? Does it seem like everything about your life is dead? Your relationships are non-existent, and when you take a look at your finances, it's dead too. You're barely making it and getting by. All hope for your life has gone out the door. Could it be that it is God who has set you in the middle of this valley called depression?

Verse 3 says, "He asked me, 'Son of man, can these bones lives?'" God is asking you, is there hope for your situation? If you're anything like Ezekiel, you would probably answer God the same way, "O Sovereign Lord, you alone know." Then he said to me, "Prophesy to these bones and say to them, 'Dry bones, hear the word of the Lord! This is what the Sovereign Lord says to these bones: I will make breath enter you, and you will come to life. I will attach tendons to you and make flesh come upon you and cover you with skin; I will put breath in you, and you will come to life. Then you will know that I am the Lord.'"

Just like God told him to prophesy to the bones, God is telling you to prophesy to everything that looks dead in your life. Open up your mouth and say to your bank account, "Bank account, I command you to come back to life in Jesus' name. I command money to come from the east, come from the west, come from the south, and come from the north and hit my bank account in the name of Jesus." Prophesy over your children's father: "I thank You, Father, that according to Isaiah 43, You are doing a new thing in my children's father's life, and I decree and declare that You are creating in Him a new heart and renewing a right spirit in him in Jesus' name. I declare that my children's father's heart is turning back to his children, and this will be the week he will reach out to me and ask to see his children for the first time. I declare that God is removing the scales off his eyes, restoring his soul, giving him a heart that would love, honor, and protect his children in Jesus' name."

Prophesy that depression is breaking off you, and you are entering into a new season, a season of more than enough, a season of overflow and prosperity. Begin to declare, "I will not die but live in Jesus' name." As you continue to read the story of the valley of dry bones, you will see that as he prophesied like he was commanded, God put the bones back together, and breath entered them, and they came to life and stood on their feet. I don't know about you, but I'm getting excited about this new thing God is already doing in your life. As you begin to prophesy and speak the opposite of what you see in your situation, God is going to bring everything back in your life together in ORDER. Did you catch that? God is a God of order, so, first, He's going to take you through a breaking season where He breaks old religious mindset and behavior patterns that are getting you no results. He's going to break how you think about money and prune out the relationship that's no longer serving you. He's going to break you in order to build you again, but this time, you will be built on the right foundation, and then you will know that this was the Lord's doing.

How to tap into this new thing God is doing in your life:

1. Submit yourself to God.

2. Read your Bible every day.

3. Ask God to remove the scales off your eyes and open your eyes and ears to understand.

4. Begin to praise and worship God. Make it a habit of dwelling in His presence.

5. Speak life over your situation. Job 22:28 says, "You shall decree a thing, and it shall be established unto you." Write out daily decrees and declarations you will begin to say over your life each and every day.

6. Break the religious mindset by not only praying for your situation to change but also putting some work behind your prayers. "Prayer changes things, but *work* rearranges things."

7. Invest in yourself. Read books that will help you grow spiritually. Hire coaches and mentors that will help you get to the next level. Attend events and conferences that will help to expand your mind. When you want something different, you have to do something differently.

ABOUT THE AUTHOR

Author Taquila Coleman knows what it is to feel like all is lost, but instead of wallowing in the pain and losing her faith, she reclaimed her life and turned her struggles into a mission.

Her book *From Depression to Deliverance* details her journey from an abandoned, young, pregnant mother-to-be to a strong, independent woman, who lives a life filled with faith, hope, and an abundance of love for herself, her child, and single mothers and their children all over the world.

Now she devotes her time to helping other women move past the heartache and depression and build a solid foundation for themselves and their families.

To learn more about Taquila, her mission, or her journey, visit her website here: www.taquilacoleman.com

Made in the USA
Middletown, DE
06 November 2020